Australia

Author	Ellen Sussman
Illustrator	Barb Lorseyedi

EP043 ©Highsmith® Inc. 1999, 2003, 2007
W5527 State Road106, P.O. Box 800
Fort Atkinson, WI 53538

Table of Contents

The Hands-on Heritage series has been designed to help you bring culture to life in your classroom! Look for the "For the Teacher" headings to find information to help you prepare for activities. Simply block out these sections when reproducing pages for student use.

Early Exploration

In the early 1600s, Dutch navigator Willem Jansz sailed from Java in Indonesia and landed at the far northeastern tip of Australia. He is thought to be the first European to set foot in Australia. He thought the prospects for settlement and finding treasure were not very promising.

Encountering unfriendly natives, Jansz advised his superiors against staying. Over the next 35 years, other explorers found the same conditions. In 1642, the Dutch sent explorer Abel Tasman from Java to take another look. He discovered the land which is now known as Tasmania, as well as New Zealand and the Fiji Islands.

The first British sailor known to have landed in Australia was William Dampier, who went ashore at King Sound in 1688. He was as discouraged as Jansz and sailed away.

Australia remained undisturbed until 1770, when Captain James Cook, on his way back to England after a long voyage, steered his ship into a natural harbor on the Pacific Coast just south of present-day Sydney. He and his crew sailed north, following the eastern coastline. Before sailing back to England, Cook claimed the eastern half of Australia for the king of England.

Project
Write and perform short skits about Australia's early explorers.

Materials
- encyclopedias and other reference materials about individual explorers
- pencil
- paper
- costumes and props as needed

Directions
1. Form a small group, and choose an early explorer to research.
2. Write a script, including dialogue, that describes the explorer's journey and experiences as he comes to Australia. Make arrangements for any costumes and props needed to perform the skit.
3. Present the skits for another class.

Exploration Voyages

The early explorers sailed many miles from their European homes to the sea coasts of Australia. Even though their journeys were filled with hard work, they experienced many new and exciting adventures during their explorations.

Take a voyage of your own as you learn about the land of Australia. Create your own ship and use it to chart your progress across the ocean waves to a world of exciting discoveries.

For the Teacher
Create an interactive bulletin board that records the progress of your class study of Australia.

Materials
- yarn in a variety of colors
- blue bulletin board paper
- Ship Pattern (page 5)
- colored pencils, markers, or crayons
- scissors
- thumbtacks

Directions
1. Divide the class into exploration teams. Copy one Ship Pattern per team. Have each team color and cut out its ship and name it.
2. Cover the bulletin board with paper. Using a different color of yarn for each team, tack or staple "waves" the length of the board.
3. Tack the ships to one side of the board. Move the ships across the waves as the study of Australia progresses. Encourage competition by awarding inches of movement for winning classroom challenges. Plan a special prize for the exploration team that reaches Australia first!

Classroom Challenges
- Use the Glossary (page 48) or the word lists from Customs and Language (page 29) for a Vocabulary Challenge.
- Plan a Design Competition for underground houses (page 16).
- Award movement inches for Animal Games and Outdoor Sports (pages 23 and 34).

EP043 Australia © Highsmith® Inc. 2007

Ship Pattern

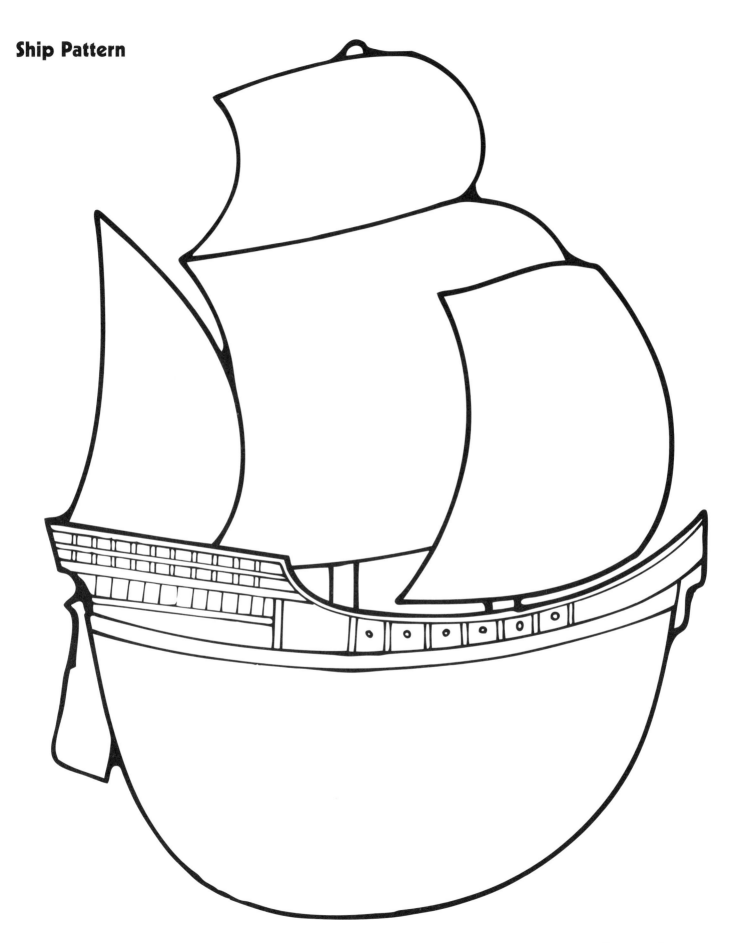

Geography

Australia is the only country that is also an entire continent. It ranks as the sixth largest country in the world in area, but it is the smallest continent. Australia lies between the Indian and South Pacific Oceans and is often referred to as being "down under" because it lies entirely in the southern hemisphere. The name Australia comes from the Latin word "australis," meaning southern.

Only a few areas along or near the coasts receive enough rain to support a large population. The most populated area is the southeastern coastal region. Australia's two largest cities—Sydney and Melbourne—are in this region. The capital, Canberra, is a short distance inland.

Australia is divided into six states: New South Wales, Queensland, South Australia, Tasmania, Victoria, and Western Australia. In addition, there are two mainland territories—the Australian Capital Territory, which is administered by the federal government, and the Northern Territory, which is responsible for its own administration, the first step toward statehood.

Project
Complete a map of Australia.

Materials
- Map of Australia
- colored pencils
- atlas or map of Australia

Directions
1. Using an atlas or map, label each state and territory.
2. Using six different colors, color each of the Australian states. Do not color the two territories.
3. Locate and label the national capital, Canberra. Identify it with a star.
4. Label the state capitals: Melbourne, Sydney, Brisbane, Adelaide, Hobart, and Perth. Label Darwin, the capital city of the Northern Territory.
5. Label these bodies of water: Indian Ocean, South Pacific Ocean.

For the Teacher
Copy one Map of Australia (page 7) per student.

EP043 Australia © Highsmith® Inc. 2007

Capital Cities

Each of the six states and two territories in Australia has its own capital city. Each capital serves as the region's political, commercial, industrial, and cultural center. The cities all share some characteristics; for example, all of them are located near natural harbors or the seacoast. However, each city also has its own unique features, sights, and landmarks.

Sydney is the capital of New South Wales and is the country's largest city. It was the host for the 2000 Olympics. Melbourne, a dignified and elegant city, is the capital of Victoria. It hosted the 1956 Olympics. Adelaide, a lovely, quiet city, is the capital of South Australia. Perth, host for the America's Cup sailing races for four years, is the capital of Western Australia, and Brisbane is the capital of Queensland. Tasmania's capital is Hobart.

The federal government administers the Australian Capital Territory, which is similar to the District of Columbia in the United States. Its capital is Canberra. Darwin is the capital of the Northern Territory.

Project
Create a travel brochure for your favorite Australian capital.

Materials
- resource books, travel books, and pictures of Australia's capital cities
- large wall map of Australia
- large stickers
- white construction paper
- colored markers

Directions
1. Use resources to gather interesting information about Australia's capital cities.

2. As a group, locate the cities on the map and mark their locations with stickers. Have a class discussion, sharing what you have discovered about each city.

3. Using construction paper and markers, design a travel brochure to encourage people to visit your favorite capital city. Include colorful illustrations and written information about the city's history. Write about what a tourist might want to see.

EP043 Australia© Highsmith® Inc. 2007

Sydney

Sydney, Australia's oldest and largest city, is the capital of New South Wales and the gateway to Australia. Most visitors enter and leave the country through Kingsford Smith International Airport. The metropolitan area has a population of about 4.3 million people. Residents of Sydney are known as Sydneysiders.

Sydney is located on a beautiful, deep harbor called Sydney Harbour. Two premier landmarks of the city are the Sydney Harbour Bridge, completed in 1932, and the spectacular seashell-shaped Opera House, built in 1973. Both of these magnificent landmarks are located on Sydney Harbour. The "billowing sails" roof of the opera house is made of concrete covered with gleaming white tiles. Many architects consider it one of the finest buildings constructed during the twentieth century. It has facilities for concerts and theater as well as operatic performances.

Project
Create a crayon resist picture of the Sydney Opera House while listening to an opera performance.

Materials
- white art paper
- pictures of the Sydney Opera House
- watercolor paints
- paintbrush
- construction paper
- glue
- video or audio recording of an opera performance

Directions
1. After studying pictures of the Sydney Opera House, use crayons to draw a heavy outline of the famous building on art paper. Add details.
2. Brush entire picture with a watercolor wash and allow to dry.
3. Use glue to mount on construction paper for display.

For the Teacher
While students are creating their opera houses, play a recording of an operatic performance. Have them pay careful attention to identify the different voice ranges.

Climate and Seasons

Australia receives most of its moisture as rain. Snow falls only in Tasmania and the Australian Alps. About one-third of the country is desert and receives less than 10 inches (25 cm) of rain per year. Much of the rest of the country gets less than 20 inches (51 cm) of rain annually, making it difficult to grow crops without irrigation. The east coast of Queensland is the wettest part of the continent and may receive as much as 150 inches (381 cm) of rain per year. The unequal rainfall in Australia is a major feature of its climate. The interior is dry most of the year, while the rain forests along the northeast coast receive plenty of rainfall and are green year round.

Australia is located in the southern hemisphere. Therefore, its seasons are opposite from areas that are located in the northern hemisphere. The southern part of the continent has four distinct seasons. Winter, the wettest and coolest season, lasts from June through August. Summer, the hottest and driest season, lasts from December through February.

Project
Use the Internet or newspaper weather section to check daily temperatures in Sydney, Australia, and compare them with your city's temperature.

Materials
- Internet access
- Weather Comparison Chart
- newspaper weather section
- scissors
- glue
- pencil

Directions
1. Cut out your weather chart and separate the weather symbols.
2. Using the Internet, go to www.yahoo.com and click on weather. Search the weather for Sydney, Australia. Choose Fahrenheit or Celsius and record the day's high temperature on your chart.
3. Glue the appropriate weather symbol onto the chart to record weather conditions. Repeat for your hometown. Complete the chart for one week.
4. Answer the following questions on a separate sheet of paper: a) What is the weather pattern? b) Is there a major difference between the weather in Sydney and the weather in your hometown? c) Is the season in Sydney opposite the season in your city? d) Based on your findings, where would you prefer to be at this time—in Sydney, Australia, or in your hometown? Explain your reasons.
5. Conduct a similar comparison between Sydney and another Australian city.

For the Teacher
Copy one Weather Comparison Chart (page 11) per student.

Weather Comparison Chart

	Monday	Tuesday	Wednesday	Thursday	Friday
My Home-town	Temp.:	Temp.:	Temp.:	Temp.:	Temp.:
Sydney, Australia	Temp.:	Temp.:	Temp.:	Temp.:	Temp.:

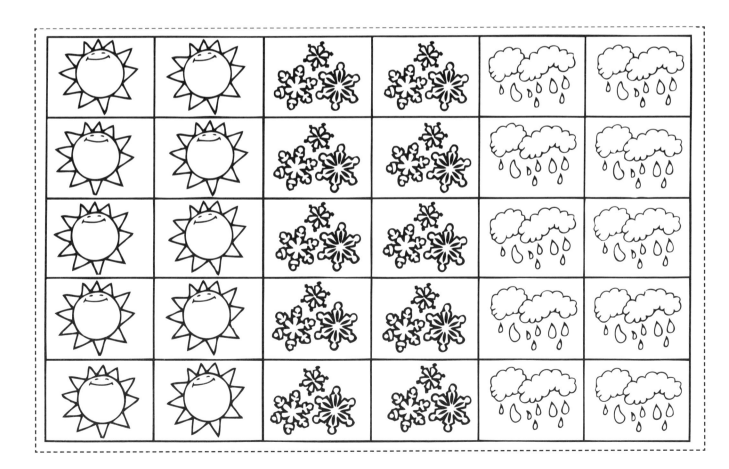

The Great Barrier Reef

One of Australia's top tourist attractions is the Great Barrier Reef. A natural wonder that stretches for more than 1,420 miles (2,300 km) along the northeast coast of Queensland, it is the largest coral reef in the world. Coral reefs are formed by tiny creatures called polyps. When polyps die, their outer skeletons are left behind. This is known as coral. Other polyps become attached to these skeletons and when they die, their skeletons add to the reef. This is how a coral reef grows.

The Great Barrier Reef is composed of about 400 species of coral in many shapes and colors. It is also home to about 1,500 different species of fish and other creatures, including sponges, starfish, crabs, sea urchins, sea cucumbers, turtles, and clams. It is the world's largest marine park. It is so large that it is the only living thing on Earth that can be seen from space!

Lots of sunshine, sandy beaches, a variety of wildlife, and ideal conditions for many water sports make this region Australia's most popular tourist attraction.

Materials
- Internet access
- The Great Barrier Reef Project Page

Directions
1. Divide into groups of three or four students.
2. Select a search engine and locate Web sites on the Great Barrier Reef. Many sites provide outstanding underwater color photography for a virtual trip to the Great Barrier Reef.
3. Take notes on fascinating facts you read about your underwater adventure. What species of fish did you see? What water sports are popular in the area of the Great Barrier Reef?
4. After you have completed your research, choose a group project from The Great Barrier Reef Project Page.

For the Teacher
Copy one The Great Barrier Reef Project Page (13) per group. Make sure all groups have access to the Internet.

EP043 Australia © Highsmith® Inc. 2007

The Great Barrier Reef Project Page

Take a virtual trip to the Great Barrier Reef on the Internet, then choose and complete a project to learn more about the Great Barrier Reef.

Photo Album

"Bring your camera" and capture some of the beautiful underwater color of the Great Barrier Reef. Select three or four underwater scenes from your Internet journey to print, or find color photographs in nature magazines to cut out. Create a photo album of your underwater journey and write a descriptive caption under each photo. Make a cover for your album.

Sea Life Dictionary

Create a sea life picture dictionary. On individual pages write definitions and create illustrations or use photographs for each of the following species of sea life: sponges, starfish, crabs, sea urchins, sea cucumbers, turtles, clams, and coral. Add others if you wish. Mount each page on colored construction paper and arrange in alphabetical order. Bind or staple your pages together.

Travel Poster

Make a travel poster to entice people to visit Australia and the Great Barrier Reef. Use a large sheet of colored construction paper. Think of a short slogan or message and use large, bold letters. Illustrate your poster with exciting and inviting pictures of this region.

Sheep Stations

Sheep were passengers on the first ship of European settlers that arrived from Great Britain in 1788. By the early 1800s, Australians had discovered that Australia's wide open spaces of dry grazing land were too poor for growing crops but are ideal for raising sheep. At about this time, there was a demand for wool in Britain and sheep ranching became an important industry in Australia. The growing wool industry brought many new settlers.

There were as many as 180 million sheep in Australia in 1990. Due to a decline in the wool market, that number has decreased to about 115.8 million sheep today. Yet Australia is still the world's largest producer and exporter of wool, accounting for about 30 percent of the world's production of wool.

Out of every 100 sheep, 80 are pure Merinos. This is a breed of Spanish origin and is prized for its fine quality of wool. About 20 of every 100 sheep are crossbreeds—mostly Border Leicesters bred with Merinos to produce a high quality of meat. The raising of sheep for both wool and meat is one of Australia's chief economic activities. Most sheep farmers also raise cattle and grow wheat.

Project

Select a project from the Wool Project Page to learn more about wool and how it is used.

Materials

- Wool Project Page
- wool yarn scraps
- cardboard
- wool fabric samples
- pinking shears
- articles of woolen clothing
- mail-order clothing catalogs
- scissors

For the Teacher

Copy one Wool Project Page (15) per student.

Wool Projects

Yarn Collage

Gather leftover wool yarn. (A local yarn shop might be willing to donate yarn.) Cut into lengths of about one yard (1 m). Using cardboard and glue, create designs with yarn by making concentric circles, zigzags, braids, or other creative shapes. Use five to six colors of yarn per project.

Catalog Search

Bring in a selection of mail-order clothing catalogs. Search for items made from wool. Cut out the descriptions with photographs. Mount on paper and display on the bulletin board to show a variety of clothing items and listings of types of wool—merino, lambswool, cashmere, shetland, and so on.

Fashion Show

Wear an article of clothing made from wool or a wool blend. Have a fashion show modeling sweaters, slacks, skirts, wool ties, socks, gloves, coats, and jackets.

Fun with Fabric

Gather samples of wool fabric in a variety of colors and patterns—stripes, checks, plaids, and so on. (Local tailors and seamstresses are a good source for small fabric swatches.) Use pinking shears to cut pieces so they will not unravel. Examine the different textures with your fingers. Create a class mural of a sheep using the swatches of wool to make an interesting pattern.

Fascinating Fact

In 1796, a few Merino sheep were shipped to Australia from South Africa. Captain John Macarthur bought three rams (males) and five ewes (females). He pioneered wool production in Australia, and became known as the "father of the Australian wool industry." In 1807, the first shipment of fine wool was sent to England where it sold for high prices.

Coober Pedy

Coober Pedy is known as the "Opal Capital of the World." It is one of Australia's oldest and largest opal mining towns, located in the Outback of South Australia. The name comes from an Aboriginal term meaning "white man's hole in the ground," because the town has very few buildings that are above ground. Many miners and their families live in houses built underground. Subterranean (underground) living is one of the best forms of protection from the intense heat of Australia's Outback. The town of Coober Pedy also has stores and hotels underground.

The underground houses are similar to above-ground houses and may have several rooms. They are equipped with running water and electricity. However, because they are underground, the rooms do not have any windows.

Project
Become an Australian architect and design and furnish an underground house.

Materials
- books on architecture
- home furnishing books or catalogs
- paper
- pencil
- colored pencils
- ruler

Directions
1. Brainstorm ideas about what features would be necessary in an underground home. How would you enter? How would the house be lit? Could you grow indoor plants?

2. Use resources to become familiar with architectural drawings and to get furnishing ideas.

3. Design your underground home and decide how it will be furnished. Use colored pencils to complete your home design.

    EP043 Australia © Highsmith® Inc. 2007

Uluru (Ayers Rock)

Ayers Rock is called Uluru ("great pebble") by the Aboriginals. It is located in Alice Springs southwest of the Northern Territory—part of the Outback in central Australia. It has numerous small caves covered with rock paintings created long ago by Aboriginal artists.

The rock rises 1,142 feet (348 m) above the sandy plains, and is actually the top of a buried mountain range. It is a 6-mile (9.6-km) walk around the entire base of this huge mass of sandstone. The rock glows red during sunrise and sunset from the iron in the sandstone.

Explorer William Gosse visited Uluru in 1873 and decided to call it Ayers Rock after the governor of South Australia, Sir Henry Ayers. In 1985, the land around the rock was returned to its traditional Aboriginal owners, the Mutijula people, who now manage the Uluru-Kata Tjuta National Park.

For the Teacher

Project
Hike a 6-mile (9.6-km) route to experience the size of Ayers Rock.

Materials
- local street map
- pedometer
- water bottle

Directions
1. As a class, plan a 6-mile (9.6-km) circular walking route. Have students:
   - use a street map to determine a route, or
   - calculate how many times they would need to circle the school grounds to walk 6 miles
   - use a pedometer to measure distance as they walk
2. Plan a class hike. Tell students to imagine they are walking around the base of Ayers Rock. Remind students to wear good walking shoes and carry bottles of water.

Find Out More
Investigate these other interesting sites in Australia.
- Southwest National Park in Tasmania
- Kakadu National Park in the Northern Territory
- Flinders Chase National Park on Kangaroo Island in South Australia
- Dandenong Ranges in Victoria
- The Olgas in the Northern Territory
- The Twelve Apostles in Victoria

Plants and Trees

Two kinds of native trees, eucalyptus (or "gum") and acacia (or "wattle"), dominate Australia's landscape. But many other types of trees and varieties of plants are found in Australia. Palm and grass trees and some cone-bearing needleleaf trees such as the kauri pine and bunya pine grow well in Australia's climate. Small shrubs called saltbushes grow in dry areas. Livestock feed on their salty leaves.

There are more than 600 species of acacia trees that bear their seeds in pods. Many have brilliant yellow flowers. The boab (Australian baobab) tree which grows in northern Western Australia has a bulb-like trunk that can measure 33 feet (10 m) around! The bottle tree has a trunk that looks just like a bottle and is planted in the dry northeast regions for shade.

Project
Work in groups to create a booklet, chart, or display titled "The ABC's of Australia's Plants and Trees."

Materials
- resource and reference books
- paper
- stapler or tape
- crayons, colored markers, and other art media

Directions
1. Form groups of four or five. Decide what type of project your group will do—a booklet or scrapbook, chart, mural, or other visual presentation.

2. Research and create a list of plants and trees. Complete a visual project titled "The ABC's of Australia's Plants and Trees" that includes the following:
   - a list of plants and trees arranged in alphabetical order
   - one or two descriptive sentences about each plant or tree
   - an illustration to accompany each description, using art media of choice

3. Display your projects and invite another class to view completed works.

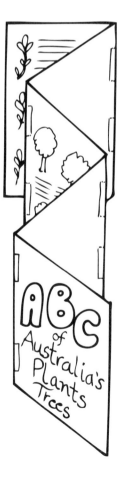

Eucalyptus Trees

Eucalyptus is the name of a group of trees native to Australia. The trees are useful for their gum, timber, and oil. Eucalyptus trees grow best in warm climates that have alternating wet and dry seasons.

In Australia, the timber of eucalyptus trees is used extensively for ship building, railroad ties, fences, piers, and telegraph poles. The jarrah variety has red wood much like mahogany. Mature leaves are long, narrow, leathery, and contain a valuable scented oil that is used to kill germs. These trees also provide food for koala bears and their cubs, who make their home in the tree branches.

Many Australians call eucalyptus trees "gum trees" because their nectar-rich fruits ooze a gummy substance. More than 500 kinds of eucalyptus grow in Australia. They grow rapidly and reach gigantic sizes. Smooth-barked trees shed their bark every year.

Project

Make a paper eucalyptus tree.

Materials

- newspaper or newsprint
- small pieces of sponge
- brown and green tempera paint
- scissors
- one rubber band per student
- index cards
- reference books

Directions

1. On a flat surface, open six to eight pieces of newspaper. The more pieces used, the taller the tree will be. Starting at one end, take one piece and roll it. When you reach the center, lay a second piece on top and continue rolling.

2. Repeat this process, adding another piece whenever you reach the center. Continue until all of the newspaper pieces have been rolled together. Secure the bottom with a rubber band about one quarter of the length up.

3. Cut the top of the tree into strips, cutting 4 inches (10 cm) down. Each strip should be about ½-inch (1.3-cm) wide. Cut strips around the entire circumference of the top.

4. With a finger, gently reach in and pull up from the inner part of the top showing dozens of leaves.

5. Use pieces of damp sponge dipped in brown tempera to dab on the trunk. When dry, dab green tempera on the top part to suggest leaves.

Animals of Australia

In addition to Australia's marvelous marsupials—kangaroos, koalas, wombats, and wallabies—the country has more than 700 species of native birds, 140 species of snakes, and 370 species of lizards. Many have fascinating features and habits that make them unique and interesting to learn about. The kookaburra, a member of the kingfisher family, is one of Australia's best-known birds. Its harsh, loud call is a familiar sound to Australians.

In the United States and Canada, marsupials are especially interesting to watch in zoos because the animals are not native to these countries and their presence is rare. Koalas, for instance, look somewhat like bears but are actually related to kangaroos. A koala can eat more than 2 pounds (.9 kg) of eucalyptus leaves every day. The leaves contain so much oil that koalas can go without a drink of water for a long time.

For the Teacher

Project
Have students gather facts and have a fact-finding conference.

Materials
- Fact-finding Page
- paper bag
- resource books

Directions
1. Make one copy of the Fact-finding Page (21). Cut apart on the lines. Fold each slip in half and place all of the slips in a paper bag.

2. Divide the class into pairs. Have pairs choose one topic from the bag without looking.

3. Make a list of each topic and the students responsible for fact-finding. Use resource books to find at least three facts about each topic, setting a time frame for research to be completed.

4. For the conference, have students report with their partners. Students should state the topic they are reporting on and recite three facts each. Photographs or other visual aids may be used.

    EP043 Australia © Highsmith® Inc. 2007

Fact-finding Page

kangaroo
how it moves

kookaburra
where it lives and what it eats

kookaburra
body description and sound it makes

kangaroo
body description

kangaroo
development of a baby joey

koala
care of its young

koala
where it lives and what it eats

koala
body description

wombat
where it lives and what it eats

wombat
body description

wallaby
similarities and differences to kangaroo

echidna
body description

echidna
care of its young

black swan
body description

lyrebird
unique features; habits living in the wild

giant saltwater crocodile
where it lives and how large it is

taipan snake
where it lives and why it is feared

cassowary
unique features

platypus
body description and care of its young

platypus
how it is different from other marsupials

Australian frilled lizard
how it protects itself

dingoes
friend or foe

Native Animal Species

It is necessary to have some geological background to understand why Australia has such interesting and unusual animals. It is believed that at one time all the continents were one huge land mass. About 200 million years ago, Australia became separated from this land mass, and as a result its animals developed differently from animals on other continents. Australia's most famous native animals include kangaroos, koalas, wallabies, wombats, and other marsupials. These are mammals that give birth to tiny, poorly developed babies. In most species of marsupials, the babies mature and develop in pouches on the mother's bellies. Australia has about 150 species of marsupials, all of which have pouches. One or more species live in every part of the country.

The platypus and the echidna are considered two of the strangest of Australia's animals. They are the only mammals that hatch their young from eggs. Platypuses live only in Australia; echidnas live in Australia and also on the nearby island of New Guinea.

Project
Conduct a research activity to identify some of Australia's native animals. Then play games to learn more about the habits of some Australian animals.

Materials
- animal reference books
- index card
- pencil
- drawing paper
- colored pencils or markers
- glue or tape
- Australian Animal Games

Directions
1. Use animal reference books to find the names of Australian marsupials. Compile a list of all of the species found.
2. Select one species and do additional research.
3. On an index card, write at least three interesting facts about the animal. Use colored pencils or markers to draw an illustration of the animal in its natural habitat. Glue or tape the card to the illustration.

4. Using illustrations, create a bulletin board display of native Australian animals. Add eucalyptus trees (page 19) to the display for dimension.
5. When your research project is done, choose some Australian animal games to play.

For the Teacher
Make enough copies of the Australian Animal Games (page 23) for students to decide in groups which games to play. Gather materials listed in game directions.

Australian Animal Games

Kangaroo Relays

Mother kangaroos go everywhere with their joeys in their pouches. Use a large belt or soft cord to tie a soft doll or large pillow to your stomach. Divide into teams and run a kangaroo relay race. Jump kangaroo-style to a marked line and back. The first team to complete the race wins.

Duckbill Dig

Pretend to be a duckbill, or platypus, scooping up worms, shellfish, and other animals from the bottom of a stream. Bury small plastic fish and sea creatures in a sand area. Divide into pairs and have a race to see which pair can first fill a container by scooping sand with their hands. (All containers must be the same size.) When the race is over, search your bucket to see how much "food" you scooped!

Koala Climb

Koalas are good climbers, as they spend most of their time in trees to reach the tasty eucalyptus leaves. Using playground climbing equipment or a flight of stairs, have a timed race to see who can climb the fastest. Use a stopwatch with a second hand to time each climb, both up and down!

Marvelous Marsupials

Australia's most famous native animals are the marsupials. About 50 different kinds of kangaroos live in Australia. The red and gray kangaroos are as large as antelope while other species are as small as cats. A large kangaroo can hop over a six-foot (1.8-m) fence. A newborn baby kangaroo, or joey, is only one inch (2.5 cm) long at birth. Wallabies are really just small kangaroos, although some wallabies are larger than some kangaroos!

A mother koala carries her baby cub in her pouch for the first six months and on her back for the next six months. Koalas eat eucalyptus leaves. Wombats are burrowing animals that are related to koalas. They eat leaves and grass and use only one-third as much energy and water as most other animals. This helps them survive on their diet of tough, dry plants.

Project
Create a marsupial pocket pet.

Materials
- Marsupial Patterns
- construction paper
- scissors
- colored marking pens or crayons
- glue
- craft materials such as yarn, fringe, fake fur
- fabric pieces

Directions
1. Use crayons or markers to decorate a border on a piece of construction paper.
2. Cut a large pocket shape from a piece of fabric. Glue the edges of the pocket to the bottom half of the construction paper, leaving the top edge of the pocket open.
3. Color your marsupial with crayons or markers and cut out. Embellish with craft materials.
4. Place your marsupial pet inside your pocket. Below the pocket, glue an index card that describes the animal you have chosen.

For the Teacher
Copy one of each Marsupial Patterns page (25 and 26) per student. Display finished projects on a bulletin board titled "Marvelous Marsupials."

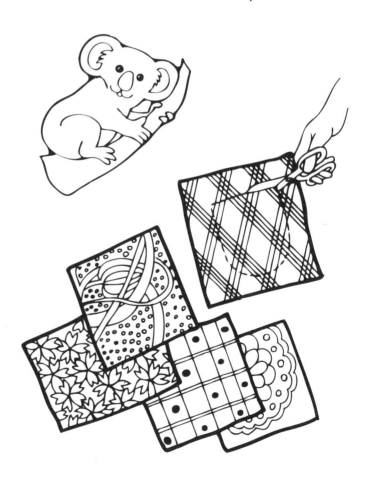

The Platypus

The platypus is a native Australian animal. The platypus is one of only two mammals that lay eggs and do not give birth to live offspring. Platypuses live along streams in Australia. They have webbed feet and broad, flat tails that help in swimming. They are often called duck-billed platypuses because their broad, flat, hairless snouts resemble duck's bills. The platypus uses its bill to scoop up worms and small shellfish from the bottoms of streams.

Platypuses live in pairs in burrows that they dig in the banks of streams. During mating season, the female builds a separate, more elaborate burrow with a nesting chamber. Females lay from one to three eggs at a time which hatch after about 10 days. Young platypuses remain with their mother and feed on her milk for about four months.

Project

Make a model platypus and create a diorama of a platypus environment.

Materials

- shoeboxes or other small boxes
- clay
- leaves and grass
- tempera paint and paintbrushes
- resource books and photographs
- index card
- pencil

Directions

1. Divide into small groups of two or three students. Use resource books and photographs to find information on platypuses and their environment.
2. Make platypuses from clay, paying special attention to the platypus's specific features: its duck-like bill, broad flat tail, and webbed feet.
3. Create a diorama of a platypus's environment. Ideas for scenes might include a platypus with a nest and eggs, a mother with her young, or a platypus swimming in a stream.
4. Use an index card to write a paragraph describing the specific elements and features of your diorama. Display the card and diorama together.

Introduced Animal Species

The only mammals that lived in Australia before the first settlers arrived were bats, mice, rats, echidnas, platypuses, and a variety of marsupials that are native to Australia. The Aboriginals, who were the first inhabitants, brought along a type of dog known as the dingo. European settlers introduced other familiar animals, such as cats, cattle, deer, foxes, goats, horses, pigs, rabbits, and sheep, as well as camels, water buffaloes, and various kinds of birds.

Some of these species have become pests and beasts of prey to ranchers and farmers. Some species have had to be eliminated or controlled. Wild rabbits have caused extensive crop damage, and dingoes prey on the sheep that are essential to Australia's economy.

For the Teacher

Project

Have students complete a research activity to learn about animals introduced to Australia.

Materials

- encyclopedias and books about animals of Australia
- Friend or Foe chart, below
- poster board or butcher paper

Directions

1. Make a large copy of the Friend or Foe chart below on poster board to post on the chalkboard or wall.

2. Discuss positive and negative habits of an animal, such as a deer, to illustrate the "Friend or Foe" concept: A deer is a beautiful animal, but it is a pest when it invades people's gardens and eats their flowers.

3. Divide the class into groups of three or four students and assign one of the animal species on the chart to each student group.

4. Have groups use resource materials to find and complete the chart for each assigned animal. Discuss the findings as a class. (Sample concepts have been filled in.)

	Friend	Foe
Cattle		
Camels		
Foxes		
Wild Rabbits		Eats farmer's crops
Dingoes		
Sheep		
Goats		
Horses	Useful in sheep roundups	
Pigs		

EP043 Australia © Highsmith® Inc. 2007

Customs and Language

Most Australian people are of British ancestry because Australia was once a British colony. When people moved from Great Britain to Australia, it was natural for them to bring British customs with them. Several customs are still a part of life in Australia today. The official language in Australia is English. People drive on the left side of the road as British drivers do, and tea is the most popular hot drink, as it is in Britain.

Some Aboriginal words have been absorbed into Australia's English language. One such word is kangaroo. Words such as "dingo" and "boomerang" are from the Dharuk language spoken near Sydney. Another Aboriginal word that is now an accepted word in Australian English is "billabong"—a combination of "billa," which means river, and "bong," which may have meant dead. A billabong is a dry river or pond that fills with water only during a heavy rainstorm.

New vocabulary emerged as settlers encountered unfamiliar things in their new environment. Notice the words Australians use for these English/American words: ranches/stations; ranch owners/squatters; backpack/matilda; a herd of animals/mob; wild horses/brumbies; Australian interior/outback.

Project

Create lists of American English words and the corresponding Australian/British words. Play a team challenge game to learn the words.

Materials

- resource books about Australia
- index cards
- pencils

Directions

1. Beginning with the words at right, create a list of familiar words or terms along with the corresponding British/Australian term.

2. Write each pair of words or phrases on an index card.

3. Divide into two or more teams and distribute the same number of word cards to each team.

4. In turn, each team selects one card and challenges a member of another team to remember the British/Australian word or phrase that matches the American word on the selected card, or vice versa.

5. If the challenge is met, play continues to the next team. If the word is missed, the player who guessed incorrectly sits down and is out of the game. The last team to have a team member standing is the winner.

Notice the British/Australian terms for these American English words.

elevator	*lift*
faucet	*tap*
crackers	*biscuits*
gasoline	*petrol*
automobile trunk	*boot*
baby carriage	*pram*

Schools of the Air

The great sheep stations and farms in the Australian Outback are too isolated for many students to get to a regular school. Outback students may be taught by their parents, but many get their lessons from a teacher who talks to them by two-way radio and/or television. Students receive and turn in their assignments and tests by mail.

Using the radio, a teacher can talk to many students located at different sheep stations at the same time. Although the teacher can't see the students, a two-way radio means that the teacher can hear as well as talk. Students must be prepared to answer questions and talk to the teacher. Once a week or so, assignments are mailed to the teacher and the work is checked to be sure the assignment is understood.

Many homes in the Outback have a special room set up as a classroom. It includes a chalkboard, wall maps, and a desk. Students follow a schedule and break for recess and lunch at the same time every day.

For the Teacher

Project

Set up a mock "school of the air" to simulate learning via a two-way radio.

Materials

- a curtain or screen
- a walkie-talkie or speaker microphone
- envelopes
- a classroom mailbox

Directions

1. Set up a screened area in a corner of the classroom to separate the teacher from the students.

2. Conduct a lesson where students are called upon to read from a book or answer specific questions. Use a speaker microphone to simulate a two-way radio. Conclude the lesson with one or more written activities. Assign a deadline for completion.

3. Have students put completed assignments into envelopes, address them, and "mail" them to the teacher for checking. Graded work is returned by way of the classroom mailbox.

4. As a class, discuss whether or not students would prefer to come to school every day or learn at home via "school of the air."

EP043 Australia © Highsmith® Inc. 2007

The Outback

Less than 10 percent of Australians live in the Outback—a term that refers specifically to the interior of the continent known for its hot, dry, desert climate. The land is mainly vast, open expanses with a few scattered settlements. It is a very inhospitable place.

Most farms in the Outback are cattle or sheep stations, and living here is extremely isolated. Large stations (ranches) may cover 1,000 square miles (2,590 square km) and may be 100 miles (160 km) from the nearest town. There are few paved roads in many parts, and travel by automobile may be difficult, if not impossible. It is not uncommon for families to own a light airplane for transportation. Some areas in Australia have a "shopping train" which brings supplies to people living in remote areas. People get on the train and shop!

For the Teacher

Project

Organize a "shopping train" to take supplies to the Australian Outback.

Materials

Items selected and supplied by students.

Directions

1. As a class, brainstorm a list of goods that might be sold on a "shopping train." What will people in the Outback need? Will the train supply medicines, household goods and furniture, food, tools, or farming equipment?

2. Have students bring in as many items on the list as possible. Large items may be represented by pictures or labeled cartons.

3. Plan a shopping day when the "shopping train" arrives at its Outback destination.

Famous Australians

A number of Australians have made names for themselves in the arts, entertainment, sports, politics, publishing, and sciences.

Australia's pop music stars include the Bee Gees and Olivia Newton-John. Joan Sutherland is a famous opera singer, while Hugh Jackman, Nicole Kidman, and Heath Ledger are popular actors. Lord Florey helped develop penicillin and shared the 1945 Nobel Prize for medicine with Sir Alexander Fleming and Sir Ernst Chain for their difficult work. Cathy Freeman was the first Aboriginal athlete to represent Australia in the Olympic Games. She won a silver medal in the 400-meter race in 1996.

For the Teacher

Project

Students will work cooperatively to list famous Australians in different fields by:

- Creating a biographical collage of a famous Australian
- Have a dress-up day and play "Name That Personality"

Materials

- resource materials (books, magazines, newspapers)
- Famous Aussies Project Page
- poster board
- colored markers
- scissors
- glue
- costumes and props as needed

Directions

1. Divide the class into five groups and assign an area to each group: music, sports, medicine, entertainment, Nobel Prize winners.

2. Have groups use resource materials to find at least three personalities in each field. Photographs or illustrations as well as written information can be used.

3. Copy one Famous Aussies Project Page (33) per group. Ask them to complete one or both projects on the Famous Aussies page.

Famous Aussies Project Page

Biographical Collage

1. Copy the information chart at right onto heavy white paper and cut out.

2. Using resource materials, complete the information for the person you have selected. Glue the chart to the upper left corner of the poster board.

3. On the remainder of the poster board, create a collage of pictures and objects that reflect the interests and achievements of your Famous Aussie.

4. Be prepared to present your collage to the class and explain the significance of the things you have selected.

Famous Aussies

Name:

Area of Specialty:

Year of Birth:
Year of Death:

Famous Accomplishments:

Name That Personality!

1. Select a Famous Aussie from the field researched by your group. Prepare a costume (including props) that will identify you as that person.

2. On a selected day, wear or bring your costume to class. Do not reveal the identity of your character to any other classmate.

3. Make a list of your classmates and try to identify the person each one represents. At the end of the day, compare lists and find out who guessed correctly!

Outdoor Sports

Australia's wonderful climate and virtually endless coastline make the country a perfect place for sports. Australians have a reputation for being fit and healthy. They like to spend as much time outdoors as possible. Many excellent beaches attract people who enjoy surfing, water skiing, sailing, swimming, and boating.

Cricket, the most popular spectator sport, is close to the hearts of Australians because the game comes from England. Some see a similarity between cricket and baseball. Cricket has a pitcher (called a bowler) and a batter (called a batsman). Rugby (called football or footie) is played with an oval-shaped leather ball that resembles an American football but is plumper and has rounder ends.

Soccer, lawn bowling, golf, and tennis are also very popular Australian sports. Four Square is a popular game played by Australian children in school play yards.

For the Teacher

Project
Students will learn how to play a common Australian game called Four Square.

Materials
- chalk
- tennis ball
- yardstick or meter device

Directions
1. Use chalk to draw a large square measuring 2 to 3 yards (1.8 to 2.75 m) on each side. Divide the large square into four smaller squares. Label the squares King, Queen, Jack, and Joker.

2. Each player stands inside one of the four squares. The king bounces the ball from inside his square to any one of the other players. The King must bounce the ball hard enough to reach its destination in one bounce.

3. The player who catches the bounced ball then bounces it on to another player.

4. If the player bouncing the ball doesn't bounce it hard enough to get it into another square, that player is out. If the player to whom the ball is bounced doesn't catch the ball, that player becomes the Joker.

5. Each player, except the King, moves up one rank. The object of the game is to advance in rank to become King.

6. Players keep bouncing the ball to try to get the King out or become King themselves.

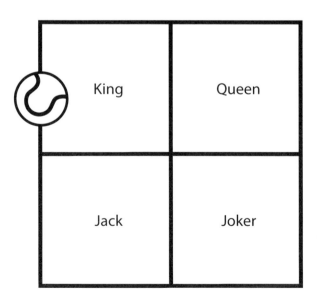

Boomerangs

An authentic boomerang is a flat, curved implement that is thrown for sport, used as a weapon, or used as a musical instrument when two are clapped together. Original boomerangs are made from wood or plastic and spin when thrown correctly. There are two kinds—returning and nonreturning. Returning boomerangs are the best-known type. When thrown correctly, the thrower can catch a returning boomerang without moving from the starting point. These are used mainly for sport.

Nonreturning boomerangs have played an important role in Aboriginal culture for centuries. A spinning boomerang can hit a target with more force than a rock. Therefore, they make useful weapons for hunting and fighting. These have less of a curved shape than returning boomerangs.

Aboriginals have also used boomerangs as tools for lighting fires, digging, cutting, and scraping, and as toys and trading objects. They are also clapped together to provide rhythm for songs and chants. Some Aboriginals decorate boomerangs with painted designs or carvings that relate to their tribe's traditions and legends. Decorated boomerangs are treated with respect and are used in religious ceremonies.

Project
Make a model of a modern returning boomerang.
(The boomerang is not intended to be thrown.)

Materials
- self-hardening clay
- pointed wooden dowels and paints for decorating (optional)

Directions
1. Work with clay to shape and create a boomerang, following the guidelines below:
   - There is a bend near the middle that forms two airplane-like wings.
   - Each wing is flat on the bottom and curved on top.
   - One edge is thicker than the other.
2. Allow the clay to harden.
3. Decorate by painting or by "carving" designs into the clay with the pointed end of a dowel before the clay hardens.

Aboriginal Art

The arts and crafts of Australian Aboriginals show great imagination. They are well known for their beautiful woven bags, baskets, and mats. Mats are woven using twine and cord made from bark, root fibers, fur, and human hair. Artistic elements of their culture can be found in music and literature.

Aboriginal cave paintings and drawings have been recognized throughout the world for their specialized skill and style. Elaborate paintings of human and animal figures were done on bark and stone using colors made from pigments in the central Australian soil. The colors used most often were yellow, red, black, and white. Designs were engraved on rock surfaces and figures were carved from stone or wood and then painted. Some traditional styles are stick-figure painting, dot painting, where dots are used to create an image, and "x-ray" painting, in which illustrations of animals and fish show the internal organs and bones. Some Aboriginal rock-painting sites are sacred.

For the Teacher

Project

Students will create a bark painting, painted rock, or woven mat.

Materials

- Painting and Weaving Project Page

Bark Painting

- bark
- acrylic paints
- paintbrush

Rock Painting

- flat, smooth rocks
- acrylic or tempera paints
- paintbrush

Woven Mat

- twine, cord, raffia, straw, dried grass, and other materials suitable for weaving

Directions

1. Collect a variety of the materials listed. To obtain pieces of tree bark, try a local art supply store or ask someone in a rural area if they will donate bark from dead trees on their property. Allow bark to dry thoroughly.

2. Use photographs to familiarize students with the unique look of Aboriginal paintings and weaving. Point out the monochromatic use of color and use of lines.

3. Set up a center for each activity on the Painting and Weaving Project Page. Post the instructions at each center.

Have students select one project to complete, or allow time to rotate through all three centers. Set up a classroom display of the finished projects and invite visitors to view the class art gallery.

EP043 Australia © Highsmith® Inc. 2007

Painting and Weaving Project Page

Rock Painting

Aboriginals hunted turtles on the islands of the Great Barrier Reef. They drew pictures like this one on cave walls. Use acrylic or tempera paints to create a scene that might depict the life of an Aboriginal.

Bark Painting

Paintings like this were done on a piece of tree bark. These paintings often featured elaborate designs of human and animal figures. Use tempera paint and a piece of dried bark to create your own bark painting.

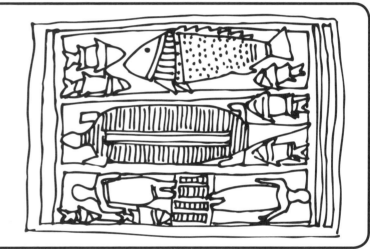

Weaving

Aboriginals used a variety of materials to create unique woven mats and bags. Use a variety of natural fibers to create a woven mat like those made by Aboriginals.

The Didgeridoo

The *didgeridoo* (also spelled didjerdu or didjeridoo) is the traditional and most characteristic instrument of the Aboriginal people. Used for over 40,000 years, the didgeridoo ranks among the world's most primitive instruments. It is made from logs hollowed out by ants and termites. This creates cavernous, maze-like chambers that, when blown through properly, emanate long droning notes. Playing the didgeridoo requires a technique of circular breathing that allows one to continue to play as you inhale.

To the Aboriginals, the didgeridoo has been associated with ceremonies called *corroborees*. These are different types of ceremonies, which require different types of didgeridoos. In a ceremony where a young male is initiated into a tribe, a very low-pitched didgeridoo is played. For times of fun and celebration, a higher-pitched didgeridoo is used that can be played quickly and can accompany festive dancing.

Project
Make a replica of a didgeridoo.

Materials
- large sheet of white construction paper
- colored markers

Directions
1. Roll the construction paper into a narrow cylinder and tape closed.
2. Use markers to decorate your didgeridoo with colorful designs.

For the Teacher
While students are creating their didgeridoo, play recordings of Aboriginal music played on a didgeridoo.

EP043 Australia © Highsmith® Inc. 2007

The Colors of Australia

Australia is a country of many colors. At sunrise and sunset, Uluru (Ayers Rock) is a fiery red. Many of the corals in the Great Barrier Reef are shades of orange and pink. The traditional paintings of Aboriginals show that they often used a rich golden yellow in their bark paintings. The long, narrow, leathery leaves of Australia's eucalyptus trees are green. The background of the country's flag is a deep blue while the waters of Sydney harbor are a rich aqua.

There are red and gray kangaroos, tan sheep, and brown koalas. The rooftop tiles of the Sydney Opera House are a gleaming white. When the country hosts the various sailing regattas, the waters are filled with a brilliant array of colored sails.

Project

Create a class book to culminate the study of Australia.

Materials

- *Colors of Australia* by Lynn A. Olawsky
- colored construction paper
- scissors
- fine-tipped colored markers
- a variety of tempera paints, paintbrushes
- butcher paper

Directions

1. Read *Colors of Australia* for a colorful description of the landscape of Australia.

2. Divide into groups. Each group is responsible for making one color page for a class book on Australia. Colored construction paper should be used for the pages. Include facts, photos, and illustrations. Arrange colored pages to form a booklet.

The Swagman

The *swagman*—a wanderer who carried his belongings in a roll on his back—is celebrated in Australian stories and songs. The roll he carried was his swag. A tin cup that hung from this roll or from his belt was used as a pot in which to boil water. In the days before vehicles, swagmen traveled only on foot, sometimes for tremendous distances as they wandered across the continent. They slept outdoors most of the time, eating wild plants and whatever they could fish from water holes or find by hunting.

Swagmen were free and not obligated to anyone. They wandered wherever they wished and Australia's enormous open spaces gave them plenty of land in which to roam and travel freely. Some swagmen, but not all, were thieves and pickpockets. The well-known song "Waltzing Matilda" tells the story of a swagman who drowns trying to get away with a sheep he has stolen. The song is a legend and is often sung by soldiers going into battle as well as at sporting events and celebrations.

Project

Learn Australian vocabulary and the lyrics to "Waltzing Matilda."

Materials

- "Waltzing Matilda" lyrics
- Vocabulary Guide
- recording of song

Directions

1. Using the Vocabulary Guide, read the song stanzas orally in groups, interpreting the words.
2. Sing along with a recording of "Waltzing Matilda."

For the Teacher

Copy one "Waltzing Matilda" lyrics (page 41) and one Vocabulary Guide (right) per student.

Vocabulary Guide

Billabong	waterhole
Billy	a tin cup used for boiling water
Coolibah tree	eucalyptus tree
Jumpbuck	sheep
Matilda	Knapsack
Squatter	big landowner
Swagman	a wanderer
To "waltz matilda"	to tramp the roads
Tucker bag	bag for carrying food

EP043 Australia © Highsmith® Inc. 2007

"Waltzing Matilda"

by Andrew (Banjo) Paterson

Once a jolly swagman camped by a billabong
Under the shade of a coolibah tree …
And he sang as he watched and waited till his billy boiled
"Who'll come a-waltzing matilda with me?"

(Chorus) "Waltzing matilda, waltzing matilda, who'll come a-waltzing matilda with me?"
And he sang as he watched and waited till his billy boiled
"Who'll come a-waltzing matilda with me?"

Up came a jumbuck to drink out that waterhole
Up jumped the swagman and grabbed him with glee
And he sang as he shoved that jumbuck in his tucker bag
"You'll come a-waltzing matilda with me!"

Chorus

Up rode the squatter mounted on his thoroughbred
Up came the troopers. One! Two! Three!
"Where's that jolly jumbuck you've got in your tucker bag?
"You'll come a-waltzing matilda with me!"

Chorus

Up jumped the swagman, sprang into that billabong
"'You'll never catch me alive!" said he …
And his GHOST (*sing softly and slowly*) may be heard as you pass
by that billabong…
"You'll come a-waltzing matilda with me!"

"Waltzing matilda, waltzing matilda, who'll come a-waltzing matilda with me?"
And his GHOST (*sing softly and slowly*) may be heard
as you pass by that billabong
"Who'll come a-waltzing matilda with me?"

Population

Aboriginal and Asian people make up the two largest ethnic groups in Australia, although approximately 95 percent of the population is of European background. When European settlers arrived in the late eighteenth century, there were about 300 different Aboriginal tribes living in Australia.

The white settlers and the Aboriginals did not understand each other's culture or way of life. The Aboriginals did not plant crops or raise animals for food, but roamed, fished, and hunted for their food. They ate roots of plants they gathered as they traveled. The white settlers did not understand these customs and took over land from the Aboriginal tribes. Many Aboriginals starved or died of European diseases. Others moved to very remote parts of the country. As of 2001, they make up only about 2.4 percent (458,500) of Australia's population.

Project
Create a mural of early Aboriginal life.

Materials
- resource books
- butcher paper
- tempera paints and paintbrushes
- pastels
- colored construction paper
- scissors

Directions
1. Using the information provided above as well as resource books, create a mural depicting early Aboriginal tribal ways of living and obtaining food.
2. Working in groups, affix butcher paper to a bulletin board or wall space. Use paints, pastels, and construction paper to create your mural.

Fascinating Fact
Aboriginals did not build permanent settlements. The best location was along a river so they could have a dependable supply of water, plants, animals, and fish to eat. Aboriginals believed that the Earth belonged to all. Berries were a gift from the Earth and belonged to whomever happened to find them first. They believed the same way about hunting and fishing. An animal or fish belonged to the person who would catch it.

Dame Nellie Melba's Famous Dessert

Dame Nellie Melba was the professional stage name of Australian coloratura soprano Helen Porter Mitchell, who lived from 1861 to 1931. She adopted a contraction of the name of her hometown, Melbourne. Nellie Melba made her operatic debut in 1887, in Brussels. Shortly after, she made her debut at the Metropolitan Opera House in New York City. In 1888, she began a 38-year association with Covent Garden in London. Nellie Melba was made a Dame of the British Empire in 1918. Peach Melba is a dessert that was created in her honor.

Peach Melba

A dessert created for a beloved Australian performer.

Ingredients
- peach halves (canned or fresh)
- individual sponge cake (as used in strawberry shortcake)
- whipped cream or vanilla ice cream
- crushed walnuts or almonds
- strawberry syrup
- maraschino cherries

Directions
1. Place a piece of sponge cake on a plate.
2. Place a peach half on top, with the cut side facing up.
3. Fill the peach half with whipped cream or vanilla ice cream. Top with syrup.
4. Sprinkle with crushed walnuts or almonds. Garnish with a cherry.

For the Teacher
Play a recording of opera music for students as they enjoy their Peach Melba (this activity would work well paired with the Sydney Opera House activity on page 9). Note: This is one of many available recipes for Peach Melba. Crushed strawberries or raspberries may be used in place of syrup.

Foods of Australia

Aboriginals, the original inhabitants of Australia, were known to move from place to place in search of food. The women fished and gathered plant roots and bulbs, while the men hunted animals with boomerangs and spears. The Aboriginals are experts at hunting animals.

Barbecues are a specialty of modern Australia. The sunny climate is ideal for cooking outdoors. Christmas Day occurs in the middle of the summer for Australians and Christmas dinner is often an outdoor barbecue at home or at the beach.

A favorite treat in Australia is Lamingtons. These are sweet, tasty cakes named after the wife of an Australian politician, Bruce Lamington. Anzacs are a popular dessert biscuit and Pavlova is a traditional dessert.

Foods of Australia Recipes

Cook up some Australian specialties. Choose one recipe, or make them all and have an Australian feast!

Pavlova

A traditional Australian dessert.

Ingredients

4–6 egg whites
pinch salt
8 oz. (227 g) castor sugar/sugar (equal parts)
1 tsp. (5 ml) white vinegar
½ tsp. (2.5 ml) vanilla
2 level tsp. (10 ml) cornstarch

Directions

1. Preheat oven to 400° F (200° C). Lightly grease cookie sheet, line with baking paper, or use non-stickcooking spray.
2. Beat the whites of eggs with a pinch of salt until stiff (until peaks form). Continue beating, while gradually adding sugar, vinegar, and vanilla, until thick. Lightly fold in cornstarch. Pile mixture into circular shape, making a hollow in the center for filling. (Mixture will swell during cooking.)
3. Bake at: Electric oven: Turn oven to 250° F (130° C) and bake undisturbed for 1½ hours. Gas oven: bake at 400° F (200° C) for 10 minutes, then turn oven to 250° F (130° C) and bake another hour.
4. Turn oven off, leaving pavlova in oven until cool.
5. Top with whipped cream and decorate with kiwi and strawberries as desired.

EP043 Australia © Highsmith® Inc. 2007

Foods of Australia Recipes

Anzacs

Bake and sample the Australian cookies, anzacs.

Ingedients

1 cup (240 ml) butter
1 cup (240 ml) flour
1 cup (240 ml) rolled oats
2 Tbsp. (30 ml) maple syrup
1 tsp. (5 ml) baking powder
1 cup (240 ml) flaked, unsweetened coconut
1 cup (240 ml) sugar

Directions

1. Soften butter slightly. Cream in maple syrup. Add remaining ingredients.
2. Roll into small balls and place well apart on greased cookie sheets.
3. Bake in preheated oven at 350° F (180° C) for about 15 minutes.
4. Check for doneness. Cool on cookie sheets before removing.

Lamingtons

Prepare Lamingtons from scratch.

Ingedients

1 cup (240 ml) butter
⅔ cup (160 ml) sugar
1½ cups (360 ml) self-rising flour
2 eggs
6 Tbsp. (90 ml) milk
1 tsp. (5 ml) vanilla
½ cup (120 ml) powdered sugar
1 Tbsp. (15 ml) cocoa
2 Tbsp. (30 ml) warm water
1¼ cup (300 ml) toasted coconut flakes
Baking pan, 7 x 11 inches (18x28 cm), 1½ inches (4 cm) deep

Directions

1. Cream butter and sugar. Beat eggs with a fork and add to creamed mixture along with milk and vanilla.
2. Gradually add sifted flour.
3. Pour mixture into baking pan that has been greased and lined. Smooth top. Bake at 325° F (170° C) for 25 to 30 minutes or until golden brown.
4. Let cake cool and cut into squares. Lift squares onto a wooden board or tray.
5. Sift powdered sugar and cocoa into a bowl. Add water to make a smooth, runny paste.
6. Using a metal spoon, spread icing over the top of each square, allowing it to drip down the sides. Sprinkle immediately with coconut.

Foods of Australia Recipes

Zucchini & Vegetable Slice

"Slice" in Australia refers to foods that are baked in a dish and cut into squares to serve.

Ingedients

1 large zucchini, grated
2 carrots, washed, peeled, and grated
1 onion, peeled and chopped
1 sweet potato, peeled and grated
1 bunch of parsley, chopped

1 cup (240 ml) self-rising flour
1 cup (240 ml) grated low fat cheese
5 eggs
½ cup (120 ml) olive oil
salt and pepper to taste

Directions

1. Preheat oven to 350°F (180° C).
2. Place cut-up vegetables into large bowl with flour and ⅔ cup (160 ml) cheese.
3. Beat eggs with olive oil until frothy and then add to bowl. Mix well. Add salt and pepper to taste.
4. Pour into oven-proof dish and sprinkle with remaining ⅓ cup (80 ml) cheese.
5. Bake for 45–50 minutes.

Bush Damper

Bush Damper is a staple bread that stockmen developed with only flour, water, salt, and a campfire to cook on.

Ingedients

3 cups (710 ml) of self-raising flour
½ tsp. (2.5 ml) salt (optional)

3 Tbsp. (45 ml) butter
½ cup (120 ml) milk
½ cup (120 ml) water

Directions

1. Sift salt and flour into a bowl. Rub in butter until the mixture resembles fine crumbs.
2. Make a well in the center, and add the combined milk and water. Miix lightly with a knife until dough leaves the sides of bowl.
3. On a lightly floured surface, gently knead and then shape into a round. Put on a greased oven tray. Pat into a round 6–6½ inch (15–16 cm) diameter.
4. With sharp knife, cut two slits across the dough like a cross, approximately ½ inch (1cm) deep. Brush the top of the dough with milk. Sift a small amount of extra flour over dough.
5. Bake in a hot oven for 10 minutes, or until golden brown. Reduce heat to medium and bake another 20 minutes. Bush Damper is best if eaten the day it is made.

EP043 Australia © Highsmith® Inc. 2007

Literature List

Australia is a large continent, geographically and culturally diverse. The following list is a sampling of the many fine books available. Check with your librarian for additional suggestions.

Are We There Yet?
by Alison Lester. Kane/Miller Book Publishers, 2005. 32 p. Gr. 3–4
Join Grace and her family as they hit the road, meeting the people and experiencing the places that make up Australia.

G'Day Australia
by April Pulley Sayre. Millbrook Press, 2003. 32 p. Gr. 3–5
Introduces the continent of Australia, looking at its geography, plant and animal life, weather, and settlement by humans.

First Peoples: The Aboriginal Peoples of Australia
by Anne Bartlett. Lerner Publications, 2002. 48 p. Gr. 3–6
Colorful photographs add to this history and culture of the Aboriginal people of Australia and the Torres Straits Islands.

Lands, Peoples and Cultures: Australia, the Culture
by Erinn Banting. Crabtree, 2002. 32 p. Gr. 3–6
Text and photos show how Australians celebrate holidays and festivals, using art, music, and dance. Others in the series include *Australia, the People* and *Australia, the Land*.

The Magic Pudding
by Norman Lindsay. New York Review Books, 2004. 172 p. Gr. 4–6
In this reissue of an Australian classic, Bunyip Bluegum, an adventurous Australian koala bear, meets up with a sailor, a penguin, and their magic pudding, which is in constant danger of being stolen.

One Night in the Coral Sea
by Sneed B. Collard III. Charlesbridge Publishing, 2006. 32 p. Gr. 3–6
Science author Collard explores Australia's Great Barrier Reef and a mass coral spawning event that occurs each spring. Intricate cut-paper illustrations capture the eye-catching colors of this underwater world.

Sun Mother Wakes the World: An Australian Creation Story
adapted by Diane Wolkstein. HarperCollins, 2004. 32 p. Gr. 3–5
An Aboriginal creation story in which the Sun slowly brings life to the Earth.

Top to Bottom Down Under
by Ted and Betsy Lewin. HarperCollins, 2005. 40 p. Gr. 3–6
Join the authors as they explore Australia from north to south where they encounter a variety of animals, such as crocodiles and kangaroos.

Uluru: Australia's Aboriginal Heart
by Caroline Arnold. Clarion Books, 2003. 64 p. Gr. 4–6
Describes Ayers Rock, in Australia's Uluru-Kata Tjuta National Park, its plant and animal life, and the country's Aboriginal people for whom the site is sacred.

You Wouldn't Want to be an 18th-Century British Convict: A Trip to Australia You'd Rather Not Take
by Meredith Costain. Franklin Watts, 2006. 32 p. Gr. 4–6
Light-hearted approach to an important aspect of Australian history.

Glossary

Aboriginals—the first people to live in Australia; originally from Southeast Asia

anzac—popular Australian biscuit

Aussie (prounounced Ozzie)—slang for Australian

Ayers Rock—the European name for Uluru; a huge rock made of sandstone that is actually the top of a buried mountain range

billabong—watering hole

billy—tin cup used for boiling water

boomerang—a curved, flat implement thrown as a weapon or for sport

continent—a great body of land on the globe

Coober Pedy—a mining town in the Outback whose houses are built underground as protection against the intense heat

coolibah tree—eucalyptus tree

coral—skeletal remains of tiny sea animals found in warm waters

corroboree—Aboriginal initiating ceremony or celebration

didgeridoo—traditional Aboriginal instrument

dingoes—wild dogs that were brought over from southeast Asia

echidna—a type of mammal that lays eggs; they have coarse, brown hair and many sharp spines on their back and sides and eat mostly ants and termites; also called spiny anteaters

eucalyptus—a native Australian gum tree with narrow leathery leaves that contain a scented oil

fleece—the covering of wool on a sheep

Great Barrier Reef—a 1,420-mile (2,300 km) stretch of coral on the northeast coast of Queensland

joey—baby kangaroo

jumbuck—sheep

kangaroo—a native Australian marsupial that carries her young in a pouch

koala—native Australian marsupial that resembles a bear but is related to the kangaroo

kookaburra—a bird that is a member of the kingfisher family and known for its harsh, loud, laughing call

lamingtons—chocolate-covered sponge cakes

mammals—animals whose young feed on their mothers' milk

marsupials—mammals whose young are poorly developed at birth and live in their mother's pouch

matilda—knapsack

Merinos—a sheep of Spanish origin known for producing the finest quality of wool

Outback—the vast, hot interior of Australia; mainly used for grazing

platypus—a mammal that lives only in Australia; the platypus along with the echidna are the only mammals that lay eggs

sheep station—a huge ranch, usually in the Outback, consisting of as many as 25,000 sheep

squatters—people who settle on land they want to own

swag—bedroll

swagman—a wanderer (tramp or hobo)

territories—lands that belong to a country

tropical—anything to do with the area of the Earth near the equator where it is hot year round

tucker bag—a bag for carrying food

wallabies—smaller members of the kangaroo family

"Waltzing Matilda"—an Australian song; to waltz matilda means to tramp the roads

wombat—a burrowing marsupial related to koalas

EP043 Australia © Highsmith® Inc. 2007